MW01033700

The Pattern Maker's Daughter

It's not easy to write narrative and lyric poems that are individually strong and also coalesce into something more than themselves—a "third body" as Robert Bly has argued. But Sandee Gertz Umbach has done such with her heart-intelligent poetry in *The Pattern Maker's Daughter*. Umbach employs a woman speaker who unsentimentally looks at (through the particular lens of epilepsy) the people and neighborhoods in the hardscrabble mill town of Johnstown, PA. Most importantly, Umbach's poems reveal how the geographic and geological landscapes have put this town in a precarious position, isolated and prone to many disastrous floods. By the book's end, we truly care about the plights of the families in Johnstown, the ones that have been able to endure the unpredictable power of nature and those who, sadly, were swept away by that power.

From granite to igneous outcroppings, Umbach knows her rocks and geological formations. Many poems speak to the pressures of the earth—sedimentary, igneous and metamorphic—and how these pressures impact the speaker's sense of the collective psyche of the people of Johnstown. In "Schist N' At," Umbach writes "The faces gathered on Dale porches tonight are sagging shale…" Again and again, with urgency and force external weather meets internal weather. Additionally, as layers of underground sediment buck and push against each other, so does the language Umbach employs in many of the poems. It is tight and muscular. Umbach knows how to create fresh, riveting similes and metaphors.

Her poems remind me of that Robert Frank's classic, haunting photograph of gauzy curtains blowing in a window that overlooks a grimy mining town, a town like Johnstown, where beauty blends with boredom, and desire is wedded to entrapment.

—Thom Ward, author of *Etcetera's Mistress*

THE PATTERN MAKER'S DAUGHTER
POEMS

SANDEE GERTZ UMBACH

WORKING LIVES SERIES
BOTTOM DOG PRESS
HURON, OHIO

© 2012 Sandee Gertz Umbach
& Bottom Dog Press
ISBN 978-1-933964-52-2
Bottom Dog Publishing
PO Box 425
Huron, Ohio 44839
http://smithdocs.net
e-mail: Lsmithdog@smithdocs.net

CREDITS:

General Editor: Larry Smith
Layout & Design: Susanna Sharp-Schwacke
Cover Design: Susanna Sharp-Schwacke and Larry Smith
Cover Art: "Golde Street" by Brody Parker Burroughs
Author Photograph: William D. Prystauk

ACKNOWLEDGEMENTS

With thanks to the Pennsylvania Council on the Arts for a poetry fellowship in 2000.

Thank you to Neil Shepard, my mentor, without whom many of these poems would not have been brought to fruition and completion.

Thanks to for L. R., my first mentor, and his boundless generosity.

With gratitude for the friendship and support of the "Best-Lookin' Cohort" at Wilkes University's Creative Writing Program.

SPECIAL THANKS TO:

My husband Paul and sons, Jordan and Christian, for their unwavering support and for their own unique creativity and inspiration.

My mother, Lois Gertz, and her tireless energy and love.

Acknowledgments continued on p. 81.

TABLE OF CONTENTS

DEDICATION

This book is dedicated to my father, William H. Gertz, the original pattern maker, and to his father, Gustav, who came to Johnstown from Germany and went into the mills of Bethlehem Steel.

"Western Pennsylvania is the Eroded Core of the Ancient Appalachians…"

From *A Geography of Pennsylvania*

Section I

"All around us, the hills hold
onto things we cannot name, the sounds
forming in our throats, little thunders
forming somewhere over their crests..."

what is a pattern maker?

THE PATTERN MAKERS

Johnstown, I want to be your Eugene Smith,
shoot Graflex still shots
of men's hardened hands, blue veins around steel.

I want to capture pattern makers from the 1950's
when they sized molds in shirts and ties,
figuring their algebraic sums in Moxham's Bar & Wire,

pencil in ear, like my father and his father lifting
their prints to the shop light, exacting
measurements of what steel will cast and harden.

Not everyone can be a pattern maker,
old men on porches tell me.
You have to see things no one else sees.

Like petunias blooming through concrete
up against tumble-down houses, rising shapes
where there are only flat lines.

Driving his Buick across Broad Avenue to the mill's iron gate
my father often said he saw himself instead turning
the wheel and taking off for Route 30 West —

climbing to the steep summit and setting up
brushes and canvas, where, for years,
he'd talked of painting the sunrise.

What did he envision beyond the craggy tops
of mountains that rimmed our valley city,
lulling us all into forgetting there was an open sky?

In the deep folds of the hills, German Lutheran men pace
silent rooms, push quarters to the edges of tired bars as pitchers
of beer lower and foam. Hundreds are sent by wives to scrub

in basement sinks, wringing their fingers under the copper faucets,
while my father dreams of the deep Black Forest,
holding his unopened tubes of Burnt Sienna.

Today when I drive the gray streets, small, bent-over
women mop porches on their knees.
Smith would have taken a picture of their wrinkled housedresses,

but I would capture the mill men posed on patios
gazing out to the Alleghenies, the patterns
of each hill, folding and unfolding in their hands.

LAST LIGHT

When all the sinks on David Street
were clanging their evening music,
mother made lists in whispers:
upstairs floorboards this week;
next week, the shelves...

Outside, the earth was speaking,
children ducking under clotheslines,
neighbors checking the reds of tomatoes,
while women retrieved the last of day's wash,
rolling up the rope in tight weary circles.

On beds of weeds, I sat in the alley,
listened to Mrs. Geisel's splashing faucets,
Minnie Miller swigging Maalox in the next kitchen,
a chorus of housedresses shifting,
Brillo sliding across the stainless.

MILLTOWN GIRLS IN FLIGHT

Glittering sandals rain from charcoal skies,
where German girls of Dale dress Barbie dolls
to alight and vault across the valley's bowl
of mountains formed by river's rapid rise.

In swimming suits and halter-tied lace wings
the milltown girls, untouched, slip by the loss
of furnace blast and steel-dust fables tossed;
their playgrounds crown a lucky queen and king.

Their hills protect from rage as well as storm.
They shield their souls in mortared shells of brick,
protect from fear when dark night fires are lit—
when whispered sighs on breath-fogged windows form.

Each blonde face glows as white as porcelain;
each porous cherub cheek is luminous;
their feet of flip-flop grace atop the crevice
of Allegheny Mountain gap and spin

across the river flask to foundry gate
and float atop the grizzled men in line—
their molten make-up and scissor clothes apply
to Barbie forms and in toy ovens bake

the recipe for gathering the suns.
Below the nuggets' steaming furnace blaze,
mill men are unaware of their daughters gaze;
their metal toes shake off the specks of dust.

JACKIE IN THE DUSK

Jackie's tanned legs swing from the banister
of her front porch; the rotten wood,
the clouds of her tobacco smoke
frame her curved hips.

She wears a halter that's been kissed
by Mad Dog lips. She is a place where mother
says not to linger—the Stingrays revving
on her front lawn and the rumbling engines
of Hornerstown boys behind the wheel.

They see me pass, my pale baby fat
just beginning its long pour over
my awkward frame. They cluck
their tongues and whisper sounds
that mix with the tones of the 8 o'clock
train whistles at the end of the tracks.

I force my legs, leaden, one in front of the other,
nursing my small self-conscious grief
down the street. I hear mother's voice rise
again in my head.

I look back.

But the boys' shadowy faces have turned
again to Jackie and the pounding
bass of her porch speakers.
I see one rough palm take the Marlboro
from her candied mouth,
inhaling his own drag
as the looming night flickers
its ribboning darkness.

What rises tonight on David Street is dust
from sidewalk chalk, siren calls,
and the tilt of a German Shepherd's

snout as it howls to the sky.
All around us, the hills hold
onto things we cannot name, the sounds
forming in our throats, little thunders
forming somewhere over their crests,
as the falcon flies out from the flock of
hemlocks into the soaring dusk.

Engines roar the wrong-way down
our one-way street while pious neighbors
jump to their feet. The Stingray spins out
of the summer gravel, Jackie's legs stretched
out and crossed over on the dash.

HOCKEY

I learned all I know about hockey
in cracking winters and sticky back alleys
where boys came to play
and try out first kisses on the willing.

The face-off was quick, and sticks
crunched the pavement. No words,
just the slide of the puck until sweat
overtook the chill and they delivered

jackets to us which we wore dutifully
with the sleeves rolled up, forming
an audience of hair on the sidelines,
the damp steps creeping through our Levi's,

trading lip gloss and whispers that rose up
into the steel gray air that laid flat across the sky.

And I fell in love with him there
because he didn't grimace like the others
making a close save or a slicing check—
because he took my hand and led me

through the streets at night, propelled
toward steep hills with stairs until our feet
frosted over in breadbags inside our boots—
our destination, dusty garages I pressed my back

into, his hands so precisely on my shoulders.
Until one day he came to my door before the sun was up,
half of the Mitzpah Benediction around his neck.
We separated only to see ourselves
as dramatic new people, to sit on other porch swings;
the smell of someone else's sweatshirt on our necks.

So I collected the brown knitted sweater
he bought with dollars saved from a paper route,
a napkin with the words to "Let it Be"
and piled it on the formica table in the kitchen.

And when he was about to go, he felt under my collar
for the one thing he wanted me to keep,
but instead found our sacred pendant pressed
into the folds of his sweaty palm.

And I could see that had done it,
his jaw unset, trying to carry it all
in one trip to his Dad's car
and his 5:30 a.m. face-off.

BLEACHING THE PORCELAIN

Your parent's voices were plush whispers in the other room,
hushed by the English brandy and the dining room's thick carpet.
You stood for your endless chores, doing the first round of dishes
and circling a pattern of suds and bleach across the bottom of the sink.
I perched on the kitchen stool, watching your shrunken
stomach up against the porcelain, your Levi's moist from splashes
at the hip, your mouth still full of hunger.

Quiet was the color of that house, the evening creaks
of the walls settling in, as you looked up to the moon shining
through the old window panes. Rising and hovering over
the table's remains were the cold words you pretended
not to hear, covered with *please pass the sugar for my tea*
and stilted spoons against jars while they smoothed
jam onto stiff bread for dessert.

All we wanted was to walk into the glow of street lights
and sidewalks lit up with the tips of cigarettes
we could follow into the length of the night.

Back then I envied how you carried all that weariness,
the thin limbs and bones of your back gracefully bent.
I held my own lucky hand of cards tight to my chest, the too-
happy house waiting for me with a circus of laughter and siblings.
I hid my soft round flesh under a loose tunic, still tasting
my mother's pudding on my lips.

Anything I had I would have willingly given—as your father pressed
a chiseled finger to the sparkling sink for inspection—
just to have been as exquisite as that misery.

STEELTOWN GIRLS

For Karen

Each day came down to an hour snuck behind
Stofko's alley, knelt on sagging concrete steps
while you rolled strawberry papers
and city boys rode bikes in Mad-Dog blush.

Other girls held flutes on stadium fields,
but we were left to watch the steel sky turn
its silver shades—the soap opera time
before parents came home from market or work.

In brutal cold, we'd walk straight into stiff wind,
hands cupped around your lighter, staring up
into stripped winter trees. Sometimes we'd pass
the hockey player with brown eyes and a stick—

a decent Catholic boy I'd lost to our madness.
As a mother now, I marvel at how we roamed
those cracking sidewalks, not much older than my son
trading baseball cards in his room.

I never told you that sometimes, in the seconds
before that first drag, I felt like running
home to stop the buzzing of the timer on the kitchen stove,
to wrap myself in the scent of mother's dough

rising there—her dishcloth folded perfectly
over the porcelain sink. Instead, we stepped
over hopscotch diagrams and planned
out lives with chalk left on the alley floor.

When I go back, Karen, I see those steps
and worn out convenience stores.
I see toddlers who could be yours spinning
on playground swings.

New girls, in skirts too short for the chill,
cross corners of Messenger and Horner.
I see their eyes, slits of rainbow glass,
a sheen too bright to look into.

SCHIST N'AT*

On Dale porches tonight, the faces are sagging
shale—no smiles like in photos gracing the volumes
of Ferndale yearbooks. They watch skeletons
of small game drift in the tired creek, and know
they are not the metamorphic glitter of the East,
just ripples of the stream joining the Little Conemaugh,
rising for dances at the Fire Hall, or a drink at Ernie's Tavern.
Carbon rich, they puff menthols, and build their volcanic ash.
Old Man Rick flicks cigarette stubs from the rocking
glider—his contents compressed under pressure
of the Iron City flip tab. Aluminum rings gather
on the stoop and coal-tinted kids string an endless
necklace, breathing in smoky circles of air. Rick sheds
layers with the dusk, dissolves into flaking schist
and the stories of a thousand loaded boxcars,
how for 55 years he turned limestone into marble.
He sits at the highest point in Dale as the hills cast
golden spells of light, filtering the last of the day's sun.
He chews on sunflower seeds and spits,
watching the shells settle into the blazing dirt.

*"N'at" is a Western Pennsylvania colloquialism for "and that."

WHAT WAS LEFT AT THE CREEKSIDE HOUSE

A single kitchen wall standing
A stove with ceramic pot
A knife that spread the peanut butter
her boys had eaten before bed.

On the counter, a roll of paper towels
Dry.

A sole family survivor of the 1977 flood, and Dale Borough resident, said when her house broke apart in the flood, her instinct was to grab her 7-year old son by the cloth of his sleeper. He was torn from her and perished, as did her older son, 8, and husband. They were three of ten victims of Dale (pop. 1200) who lost their lives in the flash flood that occurred July 19, 1977.

FLOOD FREE CITY

After the Great Johnstown Flood of 1889 the City of Johnstown Rebuilt and Declared itself "The Flood Free City." It did so again after a second major flood in 1936. After the 1977 Flash Flood, the City Rebuilt but Gave up the Name "Flood Free"

It's over thirty years since the town flooded, but on June evenings,
my family still sits down and prays toward the darkening sky—
all of us creaking as we settle into the bones of the David Street house—
the old chairs and joints of wood shaking as we bow our heads.

Outside the thunder moans and blackens, just like it did in 1977,
when we were "Flood Free"—all those years since 1936,
when the Little Conemaugh escaped the straitjackets the Army
had poured in concrete. Free like the stone of the churches crumbling

when the altars of the city broke apart in sodden grief.
In '77 we barely noticed the evening storms drenching the streets,
while two air masses wedged between the rims of the Cresson and Allegheny—
communing and planning a route no one could fathom.

Who was to know of the water's rapid rise that night, of floating toddlers
in flannel bedclothes, inches beyond their mother's grip? We were *Flood Free*,
like Becky floating on her David Street roof, her long hair a net of creek creatures.
Becky, one part sediment, one part liquid and lungs full, as time rushed

into her open mouth. Free like Roxanne, in that same Dale tide, knocking
        against the
middle school doors, where she was hurled a mile away, with breath held
        tight, and a rope
dangling in front of her reach. We watched her silent rescue, the night-
        watch above,
her body, and the overnight cleansing of objects that came up from her stomach,

the dignity of swallowed glass and iron. Today she still can recall her father
kneeling at their tiny creekside window, their house buckling beneath,
and the last words he said "Let's ride with it"…and how she did and how he
gave up her brother to waiting hands when the first rescuer came to them

and how when they came back for him, there was just the rush of new rivers
forming, while mill gates groaned into the earth and would not open—
and how somewhere before dawn in the dark forests of Route 56,
falcons knelt to prey and the mass of air was finally nudged and shaken.

Today, a meteorologist is assigned just to us—stationed to watch the clouds
forming over our heads. But we are already looking up, searching
for that yellow-green crack in the sky, listening for a distant roar, a bursting seam
in the surrounding hills—its contents we can never see until they swallow us.

STATIONARY FRONT

(On the night of July 19, 1977 an intense storm cell became stationary
between two mountain ridges over Johnstown, Pennsylvania)

For years we watched the rain swell our tiny creek
of Dale Borough. An unnamed tributary buried
beneath Berkebile Hill, it ran along the narrow alley,
its edges the worn river rock we tossed into its shallow pools,

until that summer evening when the sky opened
and broke the cobalt over our makeshift playground,
six of us looking up from a cape of Marlboro's
and sticks, barely nodding toward the yellow-green filter of the sun.

How could we have known that night it would rain
18 inches of sky to ground, the air mass swirling
and stuck between Chestnut Ridge and the rim of the Alleghenies,
the night-shift bell at the mill drowned out by its thunder and moan,

the storm unable to escape the pull of valley air—
like all of us unable to lift up and fly over those ridges—
though thousands of us drove our Chevy's down Rt. 56
to D.C., Maryland, Virginia Beach, thinking we'd left it behind,

the shelter of green hills, the stories of our fathers' lucky strikes. The voices
of those who stayed and those who came back, uncertain as the lilting
speech at the end of statements that sound more like questions we could never
quite answer—in silence when friends returned to the diner.

Folded into the crevice of those mountains, we are remote and hidden,
yet the storms keep finding us, our city's history a collective memory,
stirred when the water rises to journey down our street,
threatening all the delicate contents we have erected—

the tentative structures we build and re-build—like the creek walls
flexing their massive muscles and reflecting acid orange
and the over-design by the Army Corp of Engineers.
Only a shallow trickle runs behind a silver-chain fence

and kids toss stones from an elevated, concrete bridge.
They dangle their legs and stretch toward the echoes
of the earth's floor, but their hands will never reach the water.

BECKY'S RIDE

For Becky Lichtenfel in the Johnstown Flood of 1977

I picture her in the darkness, in flannel gown,
hair folded into curlers, as the walls of her house groan
and stretch, flailing as she floats on a piece of her roof.

We sleep through the thunder, the foundations cracking
down the block and Mr. Hoyland's fist pounding
the front door as he reports whose houses held.

Cars lift up erect and form a tower out of the zigzag
Streets; Becky is tossed into the lightning-seconds that pass
as we stand twenty feet high on our brick porch.

The sky pulses, shooting itself full of light; we glimpse skeletons
of houses we'd played in the day before. Gripping the night,
we ride our way to the morning's release of birds and cling

to rumors of Becky's ride. For years after, I'd search her face
as she stood at the David Street bus stop, for traces of thrashing
against rock, the rushing waves that flowed through her hair,

the curved mouth that swallowed a sea of sediment. In German reserve,
we guarded our Old World street of geraniums in urns
and men who molded steel—the secrets among us, we didn't pry open.

Bumping along on the bus to school, Becky only bent
her head to her books, revealing nothing to me—the taste
of mud, the thrust and force of the mad creek

the air's choking breath at her back. At the corner
convenience store, I'd pretend to choose magazines
while Becky made her quiet rounds of the aisles,

her remarkable calm, her limpid blue eyes
and lush hair in repose. Half our street was gone,
the floodtrail took one whole family, save

for the mother who held to her son's sleeper,
his body set free to the water. Accepting Red Cross shovels
we could not even attend to a trickle in the basement.

Bailing out muck from neighbors' houses, I secretly
wanted to be the epicenter, to be Becky surfacing
in Coopersdale, and to know her cold bones.

Aching to touch the beads of floodnight tears that flowed into her
brackish mouth, I would have drowned
in those waters, just to fight my way out.

JOHNSTOWN FLOOD 1977, THE DAY AFTER

The day after the flood we searched for friends,
walked barefoot over towering mud mounds, like foragers
on a strange planet, watched the return of crystal
to the sky, and felt the harsh red sun.

We pressed our feet numbly into the detritus of streets
split in two, spent wires, plumbing and lumber, all encased
in the endless swelling mud, before being hauled off
to the Fire Department for our shot of tetanus.

Disease and stench slowly unearthed, bodies hid unturned
on the river banks. What was lost was still unknown under
the strain of a fiercely blue sky; the powerful jump of the time clock

washed away with the cavernous mill doors that had measured
our city's safe passage. Steelworkers waking up in the chaos set off
for work, their chiseled features arched in a singular purpose.

I watched as they braided and tied rope, watched
sons follow fathers to cross the rushing waves
of the streets—steadied myself in the dizzying sounds
as they hollered for boys strong enough to brave the current.

Some of us never crossed, separated from best friends
whose houses lay past the water's churn.
Rumors were on everyone's lips
as we climbed, breathless up the tall mounds of brown

calling out names against the acrid air; the syllables floating
out of our mouths timidly, fearfully
as we squinted to see tiny forms appear on porches;
searching their faces, the rounds of their mouths open wide.

Girl from Tanneryville, Johnstown Flood 1977

She took an *Alice and Wonderland* watch,
a Polaroid taken on the Ferris wheel
at Idlewild Park, and five extra seconds
of breath before the water covered her house.

When she stepped off the porch and slid into the new river,
the storm drain on the corner opened its gaping mouth.
The marquee at the neighborhood theater was glowing,
outlining its Disney movie in neon flickers.

A blue light broke open as her body entered the swirling basin.
She paused to notice the houses, composed and untouched
on the other side of the street. She held her dog and felt the black
coat of her soft fur as the rushing chill clamped their skins.

But it was her hair, long and loose in the rushing
waters that floated surface-high for her mother to see.
And while the drain siphoned up t-shirt, bra, her watch
in the ribboning darkness, her mother
                              pulled.

In other parts of the city that night, a tow-headed boy failed
to grasp the thrown rope above his body, an old man sleeping,
drifted off in his mechanical bed, and the gushing streets gave way.
But the Tanneryville Girl's brown, lush hair—combed out each night
for tangles at her mother's dressing table and never cut—
                              held.

DALE PALEONTOLOGY

On David Street shirtless children dig in the sun;
they tunnel through neighbor's tomato gardens
long grown over, where Mr. Henry used to kneel
on his one good knee, telling me that no streams
are navigable from here to the ancient Atlantic—

yet many of us have tumbled headfirst downstream
when the Dale waters rose, a marker with ten names
chiseled into granite stands at the creek, next to shale
imprinted with all the weary stories.

Tammy, crumbling and conglomerate in misery,
clerks the midnight shift at the Family Dollar—
her platinum hair tied in ribbons on the girl shoveling
now to the bowels of the borough—the boy tan with dirt
is smiling the same toothy grin as Michael I knew from the alley.

Everything is history—water springing like geysers—grass
beneath my feet formed by a sequence of Tectonic events—
the day the last lot on the block transformed to
a convenience store in metamorphic glitz.

Its green silk blades transported to our skinny plot of
brown by brothers who cast off their shirts in the August
heat, carrying them on scarved heads—the memory of my father
before backhoes broke the ground—bending with his sharpened
blades, dividing the earth into perfect small squares.

PART OF THIS EARTH

I am rooted in this Appalachian bedrock,
a sliver of the earth's volcanic events.
Ancient as Africa, shiny as new slag scraped
from our hillsides, high as the Rockies
that walled us in, *(our lilting speech, our bent*
shoulders and inhibitions)
as it stretched in infancy
from Mexico to Newfoundland.

Digging in childhood holes, I see
roses grown from thin patches,
seed scattered over the cracked
alley-yards, school children picking
at slim violets. Just under this surface,
I am half Piedmont; *(half-woman,*
half informed of my senses, traffic laws,
library etiquette); my eons keep eroding.

My origins are here *(the part in my scalp,*
spaces between teeth, soft bones)
in impressions on sedimentary rocks.
They speak from layers within layers, seek
the bottom of deep oceans, travel
in shallow seas, over the history of ancient beaches,
river valleys where I'm polished and rubbed.

I am shale, common and conglomerate,
(the dirty inside of a purse, caked over lipstick
torn receipts and dried gum) skeletons
of organisms drifting. I am rapidly moving streams.
Carbon rich, organic, coal, compressed.

I am evolving,
        changing, volcanic.
(standing up straight, learning to walk
across a room, raising my eyes from the floor)
I form a thick sequence, I stack myself
eight miles high. I am a prize
for geologists.

Under great heat, violent
under pressure, I am shale changed
to slate into schist. Settling into dirt,
I am shaking the hand of who I am
becoming. I am sitting on top
of a trembling earth.

SECTION II

"...the firing synapses of my brain, fragments I capture
and silence one by flickering one."

CURES FOR EPILEPSY
(500 B.C. to the Renaissance)

Without using a sickle or blade,
when the moon is smallest in the sky:
pick the mistletoe,
and eat.

Do not offend the moon goddess Selene.
Take your robes and sleep
in the temple overnight. Hope
for Asclepius to appear in a dream.

If all this fails, live alone.

Do not have children.

Do not touch others.

Think of your falling as a dream;
enter that fall without breaking and abandon yourself.
If people say you are a genius because you have seen
the past, the present and eternity, *say they are right.*

Name the different spirits who gave you each curse
of flapping limbs and absent blinking.
Give each one a brilliant name, and pray
to St. Valentine to place a blessed ring
on each trembling finger. Hold iron
close to your chest and feel
it smother your beating heart.

Claim Julius Cesar and Petrarch as your companions.
Write like Dostoevsky.

SOME GIRLS HAVE AURAS OF BRIGHT COLORS

but mine were silver stars on walls,
tears when I sat at mother's bay window

and sometimes an odd feeling of time
over a never-ending space,

where I followed a dark hole,
layer through layer, opening

to a time before me, God,
and a time before that

until the emptiness settled
into stones in the pit of my stomach

and I had to touch anything;
a polished shoe, a porcelain cup,

to be sure I was in this world
before it shifted and fell.

Is this what Dostoevsky felt before seizures—
his glimpse of awe and understanding?

For years, this trance descended
while I sat drinking Mountain Dew on the couch,

drawn to the window view of David Street below,
older girls in games of rope jumped

on the cracked sidewalk while I wrapped
myself in exquisite sadness.

Conjuring up eternity and blackness,
I was moved to sing;

the gift of a brain's gray matter
scarred the drama I couldn't name

as stars sizzled and fell
about the room, settling

into dustless corners;
still light, still shimmering.

THE SPINNING OF THE WHIRLPOOL

I dreamed of the spillway last night,
  Karen, the mouth of Indian Lake yawning
as I entered its white foam, coma-like and drifting
  from the fall against its filmy walls, sliding
over the concrete that held back the dam.

The roar of the rushing water echoed
  just like it did that foggy day, but this time I hear your cries,
your calling to my dead weight body, sliding closer to the whirlpool.
  In the dream my call goes out to the wind and your response
again is lost in the roaring of the water spiking up into the air.

I see myself hovering above my body. I watch
  your tiny frame run shoeless and soaked
through the campsite cottages—
  your cheekbones set against the open gape of your face.

Knocked out and delicious in the churning pools,
  I saw the mouth of the EMT
closing to mine, the ambulance lights spinning
  against the pavement beneath me.

In the dream I look down into my own eyes,
  reach to touch the outer tired spirals
of the whirlpool that whipped around me in a glistening
  prism of color—part of my body bound and dug
into the earth, part of me bathing in a lightness more graceful
  than I could ever replicate again.

HER HANDS

In the silent basement office, she works among the impressions—
molds of people's teeth fill her desk.

Tiny fingers maneuver plaster specimens, dip sculptures
into sterilized jars with hands that used to run over

the cracking bones of the glass-eyed baby in her attic.
My grandmother's doll roams the house at night,

she told me, those times I slept over—awake till dawn,
her face breathing above me. She stacks her dried casts neatly,

the way she stacked porcelain dishes in the stillness
of her Messenger Street house—her shrunken stomach

up against the sink, while she listened for parents' plush whispers
in the upstairs rooms, their steps out the door to the tavern.

She molds a perfect bite, coaxing a shape out of the crooked
mouths she is dealt—an ex who forgets to pay child support,

a daughter who grows swan-like and tall—
all the endless gaping teeth will need wires she knows.

GRAND MAL

In my parents' old porcelain tub, water spits
from the shower; last night's dream of a boy's leather collar
floods my flesh. *Kiss me goodbye!*
I'm heading down that long bumpy hall…

at first there's just a sense, a low motor rumble,
like waiting for the rush of a train
in the distance.

Because doctors say they're electrical storms,
I believe they can pass, tempt with wicked lightning,
strong thunder, but no torrent.
And because I know even a sky of deep charcoal

can break, a black cloud can limp
off like a prizefighter to his corner,
I do battle.

In sprays of water, I grip the washcloth,
resisting the rising numbness,
the contorted fingers I see but cannot feel.

Words form in my mind, float
in disorder. Every fiber says *Firm,*
Solid, Silence,
must conjure up stasis
a nothingness as brilliant as the enemy.

So familiar his visits to my neural pathways,
I cling to cells crying and activated one by one,
signaled by his struck match.

Breathless, I scramble to undo the firings, race
to each nerve like a desperate child running
from ride to ride at an amusement park.

Physicians and philosophers once named this
a struggle between science and magic.
Water rippling over my new breasts,
I believe that too—at the bottom

of the porcelain tub—where my spent,
liquid words spill over mother's words
flowing into the drain, where I whisper
my goodbyes to the dark.

HEADWARD EROSION

(The Process of Tiny Headwater Streams Clawing their Way into Undissected Terrain...)
From *A Geography of Pennsylvania*

As I lay down for the jolts of light of the Sleep EEG,
the neurologist tells me that streams and synapses run and split
randomly in my brain. *The misfirings behind seizures,*
he says, and I can see they have cast suspicious shades on the strips of my scans
—cracking erosions that may have formed deep in childhood. The strobe of color
above my closed eyes spins and I see the patterns begin. I follow them
to the David Street house where I am 10 and lie flat on the grass,
my back pressing into the bedrock of the Appalachians.
My stomach stretches taut as the old neighborhood grinds and pulses
around me; Jerusalem's trumpets and lilacs bloom from my right and left hands
as I clench the fists of soil, my layers of sediment history—nothing
to explain my errant limbs or prickly neurons. The machine shakes the room
as I glance at the needle drawing out little peaks and valleys
that resemble my old neighborhood. They spike and race across the page
the way we ran, breathless, to the worn edges of Dale, following the wavy,
haphazard pathway of the alleys—my mind growing stunted and random.
We walked straight into the backs of garages where they held the sticks
for hockey or smoke, butting our heads into one wild mistake after another—
the same way the streams of my neighborhood evolved—with no guidance
from solid, shaping rocks—no sisters telling me where to shave
and how to cross my legs, our foundation's tiny cracks erupting.
That same year our Johnstown waters rose and gushed over the weathered stones
of Western Pennsylvania, we ignored our Mother's admonishments and clawed
headward into the grids of city streets beyond our borders—to the corners
of Messenger and Horner where boys appeared shirtless and dirty.
Love was still undissected then as the stereo records spun in our basements
and we tugged at our tube tops, pretending to understand the glances we savored.
I think of visiting mother now, how I can sit for hours in that long ago kitchen
at its Formica table, how I bite into the juice of garden tomatoes and grab hungrily
at the Polaroids she lays out before me, where I search my ancient traces, the places
where my mind must have divided itself. But all I see is baby fat, the warmth and glow
of snow igloos built by older brothers that enclosed me—the downy thickness
of my belly full of mother's pudding and the round face of a girl
who read the stars from her calico canopy. A girl who stayed inside when the sun was full
—the one who sometimes rises in the middle of an EEG—wiry and pulled taut by
        electrodes,
to study the hieroglyphic marks she produces on paper—as if catching a glimpse
of those wild pitching peaks will propel her further to a knowing that scratches
its way across the blank, vast page.

CLIMBING THE TOWER

On Pittsburgh's Forbes, we climbed the dark blue
stairwell tower. I was thirteen, then fifteen
and sixteen; mother, father and I rounding
the curve of its spiral metal bars,
our pilgrimage to reach Dr. Chamovitz.

He was the god everyone waited for
in that shabby little lobby—hours went by,
so you'd sit, go out for fast food,
come back, wait some more, listening
to his scanners thumping in the next room.

Stick figures from Children's Hospital were wheeled in,
bald and shushed by their nurses,
while I escaped into *Highlight's*, twirling
my hair until a woman in paisley scrubs led me
to the exam room—Dr. Chamovitz's shouts
to breathe the deep heaving breaths, echoing,
his face blurring as he tapped knees, made me walk lines like a drunk.

My Dad, a pattern maker, who prepared wooden replicas
of what steel would cast and harden,
wanted only a diagnosis on paper,
something he could explain at the lunch table
of mill men drinking thermoses of coffee and milk.

Mother wanted reasons, clipped out exotic mail-order
cures from backs of magazines, asked if eating enough
vegetables could have something to do with it
—the unsettled hands,
the falling down before dinner.

Under the banker's light of his office desk, Dr. Chamovitz
gestured to my breasts, spoke of puberty and neurons,
nodding holisticly to the 1970's. Photographs of my brain
lie on the table, a foggy sheet of gray mass and charcoal marks
—embedded mysteries I snatched from my file to learn who I was.

Hunkered over the images, he whispered to my parents
in hushed tones, the language of a lost sailor in unchartered waters,
while I stared out the window to the sea of college girls
on the street below, the blowing trash lifting up

into the wind as they balanced Cokes and books, perfect
in their careless bodies, their anonymous steps onto city sidewalks
I followed as we made our descent down the silent stairwell—

no more enlightened than the janitor opening the door to the smoking streets
where I'd let out my breath in choking, pent up gasps for air.

FISSILE FLICKERINGS

Shale is a fine-grained, sedimentary rock that is a mix of flakes of clay crystals and tiny fragments and silt-sized particles of other minerals including quartz and calcite. It is characterized by splintery breaks along its thin laminae, creating fissility.

The Geography of Pennsylvania

The creek edge glitters with pieces of ancient, broken
shale. I see my childhood pale filled, sooty fingers rubbing
over fossils that rode in the great floods. Crystal crumbles
of color I tapped from the rocks spin from the flickering
lights of my Sleep EEG. Black rock becomes silver metal silt,
red dots are ferric and hematite. Deep browns filled with iron
oxide are my mental guiderails, and yellow is the limonite taste
of seizures still tart on the tongue. Paleozoic green—the color
of the Laurel Hills assembles above my closed eyes, while outside,
orange-tinted creek water pushes on its journey
to the deep "V" of the Conemaugh Gap.

A matronly nurse collects the blips and bleeps of my brain
waves on computer paper—as intrigued as if she were reading
a cereal box. How could she know when the line runs
smooth I think of the shale's soft clay we formed into toy
roads in our grassless yard? That it spikes and I am flying
over the Alleghenies, my scattered neurons splintering over
tight mountain passes—the entrance and exits to this fissured
flood city—the firing synapses of my brain, fragments I capture
and silence one by flickering one.

BLOWING THE PINWHEEL

At Children's, 6th floor, Neurology, the technician makes my son blow
the pinwheel. Lying down on the plastic couch for the EEG,
his eyes dance as he purses his lips, spinning the clownish colors
of something you'd win at a fireman's festival.

He thinks it's a game, his scalp mapped with electrodes, wires rising
from his head and dangling across the room. I'm grateful for the kind tech
with pictures of smiling boys on his desk, his thoughtful gaze into the computer
screen that holds my son's brain waves. In seconds I'll know

what the hieroglyph markings reveal, but now he wants my son to breathe—
the deep hyperventilating I never understood when my mother led me
up the spiral stairwell to Dr. Chamovitz's office. His gravel voice barked
and hands clapped as he coaxed air and counted breaths,

Three more and there are tootsie rolls on my desk!
until the last exhale when light descended
into ribboned, fluttering darkness.

Breathing creates changes in electrical impulse,
the tech tells me. He knows my history, laughs
when I tell him the electrodes used to be 42 sharp needles,
not Velcro patches—*Only the ones in the ears hurt,*
I say, remembering the trips I took to this same hospital

Doctors there sent my parents off with referrals and paper instructions.
*Don't restrain the child. They won't swallow
their tongue. Beware of strobe lights...*

Staring at the spinning wheel I can see Dr. Chamovitz's glass bulbs flashing
their techno patterns, the stations of toys I marched through, mechanical and wired,
transmitting messages to bulky printers in secret code while father went out
to feed quarters to the meters between Fifth and Forbes.

With my son I share lips, nose, the smile from our second grade
pictures, and now a private space where neurons collide
like bumper cars emitting their brilliant sparks.

The room darkens as the tech installs a light above my sleeping son.
Rapid-fire, red dots ignite the air as the technician heads for the door,
startled by the jumping on the screen. I step into the glow of the computer.
Six lines spike across the page, fluorescent green threads weaving their jangled
        currents.

The pinwheel, still clutched in my son's hand, rises and falls
with his dreaming breaths, the flickering bulb hovers over us
sputtering its last dizzy rays. My eyes inexplicably fix on one straight line.

Section III

"Engines revving against the dark, and then softening in the hush of the emerging dawn."

PROSPERITY, 1952

When times were good and the mills hot, my Dad worked the crane
and raked in the overtime. On 191 David Street, the fridge was full

of sirloin and salmon. Mom said that's when Dad was his biggest,
on top of the rig all day, double chipped ham sandwiches for lunch.

At night, he'd bring home treats to the second floor of the old Victorian
before they bought the whole house. Boys tucked in, the coffee table full

of pop and subs from Coe's, my mother opened cellophane snacks—
careful not to let Jimmy, the one with good ears, hear them popping off

the Coke bottle tops. Feet up, close to the TV, they'd toast Bethlehem Steel,
the breeze blowing in from the window to the tiny brick porch,

the baby girl that's yet to be, while stealing sips of the sweet fizz—
the rim of the bottles, wet and glistening.

THE BRA FACTORY

I try to tell my brother not to call himself a "go-fer"
just because he fetches cardboard
for women shouting *"Bring me a double order,"*
who get paid by the piece.

A thin vibration against her machine,
Wendy filled 40D cups with tissue paper
and longing until opting for a little more herself.
She used to sew the fine pink bows
til the Singer's were hauled out on dollies.
Packaging's what's left and Jim hands her the least
boxes, her body buckling under the weight.

Wendy is the quietest 36C the plant has ever seen—
she can wear a skin tight mini with a halter
and never make a sound. Her high breathless
voice makes no impact among the carping yells—
the broads she's stacked up against,
the ones who have stuffed bras for 22 years,
supporting alcoholic husbands with a snap of their wrists—
simple as taking off an underwire, long before
we knew about carpal tunnel.

My brother says Wendy gets a hard time
about her clothes, what she reveals
in the factory's windowless rooms
about her boyfriend of 18 years,
how they'll get married
when he gets a steady job,
why she lives at home,
why he lives with his mother
why they've gone on dates
while six presidents have come and gone
in the White House
and they still say goodnight at the door.

My brother keeps running,
says yes to Wendy
and the other pleading eyes,
moving too fast to speak
above the conveyor—
brings back tags and boxes
stacked to his temples,
ones he knows will be left
untouched at day's end.

It's better than the hobby store—
13 years stocking inventory
till the notice. This is the union
and it's harder to lose a job
here where the hard part's already done—
cotton and silk sewn
on in China, flown in crates to loading
dock men in steel-toed boots,
to my brother prying open
the wooden folds to dangle
the lace and satin—to Wendy's silent
slip of her wrist—to the women waiting
with plastic tags, America's last
mark on the industry, pressed
in the creases of their raw
bent hands.

SUMAC TREE TRIUMPH

After lunch, Tony's boss tells him to pull up the roots
of the Sumac Trees. They proliferate the edges of the mill,
shoot up between rail lines of the locomotives, in gutters,
and between the tiny scrapes of metal.

Tony's arms are thick and tanned from breaks in the sun.
He reads mysteries over his lunchbox and calls the wavy leaves
"Pittsburgh's Palms"—pretends to open a can of Iron City
under their thin shade and squirts the juice of an orange into his open mouth.

"It's a shame to uproot them," he tells the foreman, who returns
to half-napping under his cocked hard-hat. Ed, his partner on the crew,
swigs black coffee and turns his head to the sky, blows smoke
and his thoughts up into the gray, steel air.

Tony pulls just enough of the stems so when the foreman opens
one eye, he nods and smiles. While his muscled hands leave
the long, strong roots untouched.

I CAN'T HELP BUT THINK ABOUT EVE

as I stand on the factory's scaffolded perch,
looking down to the dustless workspace
of the man with the red fire ball.

His stomach stretches the threads of his black t-shirt,
as he blows a long, urgent breath into the glass
giving way to elegant roundness.

He nods, and the woman on the crate rises
to ready the cast iron. On her knees, she bends over it,
opens the heavy black forms

as he dips and lifts, shaping the beginnings
of something she will rush to the kiln.

He has no choice but to trust her liquid movements,
her devotion to the tenuous bulb he holds out
to air and back into fire.

She offers the scissors as he sits at the bench,
sliding his work into the metal stand
no seconds can be lost

in his careful clipping, her routine of stations,
and white spaces she must move within.

I think of their fluid dance, interrupted if she took a step
out of turn, if he moved too quickly from the blazing
heat to her waiting tools.

She holds the firm lip of a fluted vase to his for sizing,
and they nearly touch, each mouth forming their delicate O's
as he continues to mold the limpid glass.

The woman rests at her crate, until his final glance
when they expose what they have created to first light,
shading it with the cups of her cool hands.

THE SECRET

They said you bled right here
on the factory floor, wiped it up
with stiff restroom towels that crinkled
like construction paper on concrete.

Hunched over, rubbing in circles,
while Carol and Ann came running—
asking what they could do, what it was
and you said, "Leave it alone, I'll get it,"
in the same voice you might have told your girls
to move away from broken glass on your kitchen floor.

Then you stuffed more towels
and Kleenex from your purse down your shirt,
to the raw wet spot of your breast
and took your place in line.
Lifted, fastened, taped,
till sweat beaded on your cheeks
and you didn't think your arm would rise
again and support the weight of your secret
gone mad, and thought
            "This is money for my children's college."

Bolted to the wall, the time clock punched
out hours you'd put in, the dirty jokes
you'd take home and never repeat.
Those last weeks you were still making lists:
a gift for that baby shower, shop for a futon
for your daughter's dorm room.
So busy being silent, you built a wall around your body.
No one could see, no one could touch.

SERVICE CENTER REPAIR

I'm driving the mechanic, trying to show
him the sound my car makes when it goes
over 60, but we're not on the highway yet,
so he talks and I listen. This car's new;
I should be home cleaning out a closet,
weeding the garden, but I find comfort
in following his directions, turning when told.
I'm working on getting outta' there,
he tells me, *Going on my own. I'm not
supposed to, but I work on cars in my garage.*
He has a new baby and a young wife,
wants to make enough so she doesn't
have to work, so they can move—
says he gets home, eats dinner, plays
with the baby for half an hour and it's off
to the garage till 11 o' clock. He's building
decks too—on the side—*I don't want to work
on cars anymore. I'm saving up for a backhoe.*
Does this work on weekends, doesn't sleep much.
We're on Route 70 now, up to 60,
and that darn noise won't sing for me, the whistle
that's been screeching from the windshield
for weeks, and he's telling me it's either
a contracting business, or in with the power
company—*you can be set with a pension at 55.*

75 miles per hour and he says I hear it now!
I let out a sigh; he doesn't know how drawn I am
to the neck of his blue collar, just like my Dad's
—everything I wanted to trade—stretching
out on the passenger side of my car.
I want to tell him not to work so hard,
that money could makes things complicated—
that his wife might find the postman
becoming more attractive with his regular hours
and the careful way he raps on the door
when the baby's sleeping. I tell him
my husband's on a plane chasing
The American Dream, on his way to a city
I'll forget until his call. I want to tell
him to play with his baby all night long—

put her to bed with a story, then stay
up late talking to his wife, to sleep in
and call in sick. I want to tell him
how silly I feel about a noise I only hear
when I go over 70; I want to tell him
to slow down, but I don't know how.

THE FARMER

Ralph took the Amish farmer out into the rye,
the beans, the strangle of tall green corn, stopped
in the dead center of the fields and pulled at a fistful
of loamy black soil. *You know I need to sell. I'm too old*
for plowing and it's either you or lots divided up,
he told the man who'd been leasing his fields, looking
directly into his wide-brim hat, judging his hands
forming a deep brown outline against a white stiff shirt.

First summer sun pressed down, bleaching the top
of Ralph's gray-sheen hair while black crows counted
the seconds before the Amish man shifted
his feet, explained in measured tones
about his wife 20 miles down the road—
the elders who'd never let him own those acres,
the rows of straw-colored life popping beneath the cobalt sky.

All that last year spent balancing bills, Ralph
listened to the man clanging the barn bell,
the steady way he led the Appaloosa through his paces
—all the daily habits he savored, stirring the cream
into his coffee, tucking the land offers into the family Bible
—staring out past the kitchen's café curtains
to the barbed wire fence—to the Amish man's shadow
covering the plump cows lazing along the potholed road.

IN THE KITCHEN AT THE GREEK BOY DINER

I push my plastic tray up on the stainless
steel as they wait for me to hand them the slip.
Wordless shrugs of shoulders
but the script they recognize;
     gyro
          souvlaki
               spanakopita
Their faces glisten with the color of
olives in the jar where they dip
their hands and fling off the juice; flirting.

But one, Christaki, is fresh from Cyprus,
his longing for the sea
a shadow beneath black eyes, silence
as the cooks translate
Saturday night bar stories,
their broken syllables lilting up
into the steam of pans and plates.

Christaki wraps pita and meat,
pushes it toward my smeared apron.
I stand with the uniformed girls,
in our starched white collars,
lined up with our baby fat
still clinging to our waist.

We learn new words
while Christaki shakes oregano
        'te Kaneis'
              'para kalo'
as the cooks grin
skinny, shining
mouthfuls of teeth.

CAROLYN CLARK WALKING

In faded print dresses,
        lumps rising in her back,
Carolyn Clark walked the streets
        of Dale never looking up.

Clutching a bag for each stretched arm
        she walked downtown to the mission
to the grocery pulling a wagon
        her long brown hair bobbing toward the passing cars.

For 23 years I wondered what she saw
        in the cracks of those littered sidewalks—
Obie, her father's face? His last blood cough
        in the dim light of their David Street living room?

He was too frail for hard labor, left no insurance,
        no notes said *"keep walking daughter."*
Yet each day she logged a marathon of miles.
        in summer, in a thin frock, in winter, a barely-stitched coat.

Neighbors on the block started, then stopped
        bringing the casseroles, and marveled at how Carolyn
scavenged for her supper, while her sister became a swan
        sprouted height and bones as she twirled a baton —

taken in by an aunt who showed her how her hair worn up
        would elongate her neck, how a girl like her could go places
in tights, her silvery wand shimmering as it leaped from her hands
        into fire at the Ferndale football field.

Carolyn keeps her sister's clippings in a tin,
        opens it in the David Street dusk to sister's silk and glitter,
and the few sashes she has left behind
        the language of all she has won:

      Conemaugh River Champion, Miss Golden Twirl
      Penn State Scholarship

while Carolyn walks the city edges of Goldie and Von Lunen,
        turning toward middle-age in a ritual step
after step, yet her eyes remain a girl's. I want to say
        they have met mine, that there is a deepness there—

or a longing where vacant pools stare down to concrete ridges,
        where experience should reflect a man's first kiss,
or one held hand those nights she scans the mirror and sister's photographs,
        their nearly identical faces mingling as she combs

out her long brown hair in the room they both
        slept in before Obie died, before sister swept up
her baton from the wooden floor and strode down
        the stairs of the double house to a waiting car,
her back flat, her neck stretching.

VISIT TO COHOES

You raised yourself up on bricks
at 31 Olmstead Street, building a ladder
from the crawlspace of your basement
windowsill, stretching to peer in at the mother
who'd banished you to a cold cover of leaves,
to see if she'd fall asleep, if she'd left a stray
cracker on the kitchen's slim counters,
or if the clock hands had moved enough
to tick-off the four-hours time.

You said you wanted to take me there,
where Canadian Indians settled in rowhouses
where father's last drunken nights played out
on patterned linoleum while cans dwindled
in the pantry, waiting for your mother to find
courage to walk to the store—to forget the part
in her hair was off center, or that her dress might blow
taking the hill in heels past Cohoes Textile Mill
where Cherokee-blood women smoke
outside on morning breaks.

Brown faces looked out from behind the door
asking what we wanted. I felt I had to say,
He lived here. He's a poet, and things happened
like they are happening to you now—
the poverty we didn't speak of as they invited
us in, gesturing at your Mohawk-dark skin
as you remembered the running out
of food stamps and your mother's trick of sending
her small son to Jimmy's Store for pity.

Instead we talked of architectural lines,
of original windows and faded brick—the tin
ceiling above the room where your father
counted coins over bottles of Schlitz
and you read *Moby Dick* under a dim bulb,
where we stood that day in silence
with strangers, your black eyes piercing
everything you saw.

'PANASOMU' PEOPLE

(In Rusyn Language, meaning; people like us)

In fog of their magic forests,
the Carpathian Mountain people
laid low in their dirt beds
formed a barrier between countries—
a Hungarian king who hypnotized
them into silence, revolutions hollow
and long as a werewolf's call
and then stillness, and still no food.

One million people forced from their villages
Of *Sucha* and *Lemko*, dispersed,
until their neighbor became Polish
their past forgotten rapes and beatings.
30,000 of them sit down to dinner
in Western Pennsylvania, bless hams
and answer grandchildren's questions:
"Who are we?", "Where do we come from?"
with *"Slovak, Ukranian, Russian..."*

Those were the only choices
the soldiers offered, knocking at the straw mats
of Carpathian shacks, in search of something
they could write in their shuffling papers.
"We are Rusyn!" they sang,
slap happy serfs in their Byzantine
aprons and brocaded collars,
they were slaves but they knew
who they were—

Rusyns who crooned the clear sweet notes
of their national anthem, one soul wound
into the tight strings of zithers
played after days spent sheaving
wheat, carrying stalks to priests
who might find favor in a son.

A people still afraid of the wind,
the night's howling,
and the evil red eye—
the village sleeps in turns,
one man asleep, one fanning
the russet flames of fires
leaping from their black
beautiful wood.

THINKING OF AN OLD BOYFRIEND
AFTER SEEING A '79 CHEVY LASER

…how I climbed out the window that night from my canopy bed,
to let your engine take us down Route 70 West,
and I how I didn't want to believe the world
could open up like that, the wide earth stretching
and weather shooting straight from the hovering sky
to the spiny cracks of your windshield.

When we passed the Indiana State line I asked you to take me
back to the hills and curving valleys, the intimate
streets I navigated with two hands on the wheel.
You stared straight ahead, like you could drive on
that way forever, absently tapping your cigarette in the ash tray,
my hand dug into the muscles of your Levi's.

When Indiana came and passed, I saw my father
back on the David Street front porch, refusing
to shake your hand, how he said the stint in Juvenile Hall tainted
your intentions, how the wheels of your car were just a bit
too jacked up. He said it was something in your shining eyes,
but I know it was your stereo pounding in the night as you pulled
up and idled at the back lilac tree.

The window stuck and creaked, and today a part of me
can still feel the freedom of that jump to the patio—
the chill of the breeze under my fluttering nightgown.

For a moment before you turned around that night
I wondered what my father saw in the slits of your eyes,
in your ruddy, skin. I prayed over the dwindling
gas tank needle, held my breath as the highway narrowed
its lanes and merged into the wavy mountain passes—I watched the clock
hands of the dash move fitfully—my clenched bones easing only as I lowered
the bedroom window and nestled my long blonde hair
into the calico of my print bedspread.

As I drifted off to sleep, I could hear your engine revving
against what was left of the dark, and then softening
in the hush of the emerging dawn.

WHEN MY PARENTS FOUGHT

We found the morning newspaper full of holes,
apartment ads my Dad had cut out.
At breakfast, I stared straight through the gaps
in the classifieds as mother held up
the paper to catch first morning light—
the kitchen table still full of crumbs and spoons,
the tiny cup that held my father's 5 A.M. egg.

Dad returned at three, turned on the TV
while mother quietly carried the
stepladder from room to room, searching
for dirt that settled into the floorboards,
"You don't even know it's there," she'd say, wringing
her hands inside the rubber gloves, satisfied
with her rag full of imagined dust.

Three weeks of cutting holes
and they can't remember the reason.

It could have started on the porch,
mother down on her knees scrubbing,
the morning we were to go to Fun World,
with sandwiches to make and coolers to pack with ice.
Or maybe she heaved an absent sigh when he talked
about the pattern shop, how he stood all day behind a wooden slab
table, calculating the corners and edges of huge steel plates,

till they ended up slogging through the hours
nursing their small grudges, mother
not accepting communion, me talking louder
at the dinner table to cover the unspoken words,
pouring the coffee we thickened with milk and the dusk
falling on David Street, where I'd caress the dishcloth,
over bowls, cups, plates, in an attempt to wipe everything clean.

THIS IS ENOUGH

(A Variation on Gerald Stern's "This is It"…)

It is my emotions that carry me through Deer Park, Maryland,
sheer feeling—and an SUV on a slit of road—
iced with plow marks and snow towers barely passable.
Leading me to the general store at the core
of the town; a sad-stooped building with ivy plants
growing in the window from 1963
and dust piled on sills so that I sneeze on entry.
I talk to the old lady owner who hasn't changed the clasp
of her bun in fifty years; who charts the passing of trains
across the road on the tracks, this woman who, for decades,
has stared out from the streaked glass to the raising
and lowering of gates, the blinking red lights
that hold motorists in sway.

I ask for things that are not on the shelves and mourn
for the vast vacant spaces on them. I see the soup
cans leaning next to toothpaste and little safety pins
in plastic holders. I share the woman's grief for her lost
husband who last piled on gear for a hunt in 1978.

Everyone in Deer Park is into myth! The surrounding countryside
is full of French innkeepers who study basil and collect
sadness from weary travelers' coats. Sturdy trailers
fill the length of rubble roads where Deer Park natives
slow dance after dinner in their dimly lit kitchens.

No more than Deer Park will do for living out a dreamy vision.
The old woman taps out a pattern of lost youth on the ancient register
keys. Her crinkled veins place change into my own thawing hands.
She tells me about the care of ivy and other green vines that dangle
from the cobwebbed corners. She tells me the time of the train
stops and the television line-up for Thursday though it is Saturday.

As for sadness, there are very few places like Deer Park.
Sagging with boredom and lilacs under snowfall; hearts
brooding over tourism and newly painted bike lanes.
I know Johnstown, PA and Elmira, New York, I know
steel rigs and aluminum, storefronts painted by children
to mask the empty downtowns.

But Deer Park is special—its ghost-like chill running
through the residents as they step in their frozen ground, struggle
to touch each others' storm doors, carry mail from roadside
boxes, careful not let out secrets to the February air.

Across the road, a sign catches my eye: "Handy Girls"
spelled out in peeling lettering. From the road, you can see
a room humming with women at sewing machines in rows.
You can smell lint from dryers spinning and their vents
exposed to the cold. I study the women's pale arms
bending to their work and imagine them thinking
about their chubby sons seated at school desks. I turn
from them to the old woman peering back at me from her glassy perch.
Without a groomed mountain and lake, the people of Deer Park
could vanish here. No strangers peering in factory windows,
no customers' cash to break a good afternoon's spell.

On the corner, the fire department's heavy doors open
and shut while plows scrape up bits of trash and ice.
I listen to what the mountains tell me here—that "this is it"—
it could not get any better than a town like Deer Park
and its scrubbed and unscrubbed inhabitants and hills.
It's not Lambertville, New Jersey, but I could stand here for hours
and watch the track's barriers rise and fall; letting the town bury
my enraptured body, over and over like that until spring lifts
its snowy cover and the last rites of winter pronounce their reckoning.

OLD LOVE

Worn into the swirls of the print bedspread are faded coffee splashes
from steaming cups you've brought to my drugged sleep,
the wire of your frame already wound for the day;
flight numbers and polished shoes bolting out the door.

I burrow into the body of your foam pillow you cannot bear to change;
a weightless stretch of satin, before senses wake the bones and dawn
breaks in. You leave each day an apparition I peck toward
a cloud of striped shirt and stiff cologne.

On your dresser, I run my hands over 21 years of age spots,
keys and quarters that fill the tired pottery bowl our son made in second grade.
For weeks it can sometimes go on like that—the morning ghost
and the moonlit briefcase hitting the darkened floor.

We're not the love a drugstore card contains, but sometimes when
you are gone I dive into the cedar smells of drawers, to the bottom
where the Woolrich sweaters lie; the ones from the New England honeymoon,
and marvel at all their tightly sewn threads. I empty your jeans inside out and ache
to touch the tiny creases of receipts so tidily folded in the pockets—
evidence of all the lattes and cabs; the tollbooth gates
that have lifted for your passing, without me there.

Today you come home from the thousandth trip and it's obvious
you missed the dog. I go to our room to put away the remnants
of your packing. From the window I catch sight of you in the yard,
laughing and lifting the bulk of the young lab's body like a baby
to your chest. I bring the form of your barely worn shirt to mine
and inhale what age and time have given us.

The "Being" of the Geranium

This flower I can only name "bliss,"
so shocking with its sprays of blood petals,
transforms in my possession.

Yesterday, it displayed itself against the grain
of the cocktail table like a showgirl, promising
and vital. Freshly cut and flashing its too-red lips,

it has lived many moments of being—nights
under the Chautauqua moon, days
when its color drew people to hunch over it in praise.

In the moment it was cut, it had its finest, longest
ecstasy. Its bouquet is flattening as I untangle
it from my hair, place it in my book, my purse.

If it were a wife, it would be buying new lingerie.
Its wrinkled tissues cower behind last
blooms, the buds unopened are left dangling.

As it sheds its wild beauty, it builds an interior
mystery that accompanies my silences.
When I open my book I am jolted by its color.

I linger over its silken and shattering body.
Inside my notebook pages, it is drying,
settling on its thin green stem.

POSSIBLE MEN

After Ted Kooser

There were once so many I might choose among,
running my fingers through a mess of curly hair, measuring
myself to the tall and dark, or bending to the short and intriguing.
In Washington, D.C. diplomats with foreign tongues
lapped the lanes of the rooftop pool of my building
in Speedos and carved waists. In New York state
there were IBM'ers with polished shoes—they searched
for wives like their bosses had, Stepford and smiling.
And back home, waiting in Western Pennsylvania
were all the ones on hold, Steeler sweatshirts
on stocky, solid frames—forks stabbing
at their mother's pumpkin pies. On Autumn Sundays,
they chose a girl after throwing her a looping spiral.

There were once so many wardrobes—fit for any one
of them at a moment's call—I could see myself in the embassies
I spied in at nights as I drove my lonely Laser GT up Massachusetts Ave.
I'd be wearing black cocktail, or attending a sales dinner
in Binghamton in full suit, clapping wildly for the IBM's top seller,
or slipping into a jazz club in satin to see the saxophonist
from the dating service weave his spell. And once, yes once,
I saw myself with you. And now what I have is this one person –
the one I would choose if faced with a car and a cross-
county drive—the only one with whom the words are not
snuffed out by the miles as we live the last and best possibilities.

CROSSING THE CHAIN OF ROCKS BRIDGE

I can't look out the car window because my husband
tells me we're at the muddy bottom of the Missouri River,
spilled out onto cornfields as it does some years,
and the swampland I see when I dare to turn my head
is really Fun City's 2-acre pool—Lisa Kohler
choking me at the 5-foot marker.

Silt and nutrients feed here—the best farmland –
he tells me, but I'm at summer's horse camp,
twelve and puffing up the Allegheny Hill
on a dare to swim the empty pool at night.
The water barely stirring, I knew it could suck
me in if I didn't' take two steps, then skip,
then run back down the hillside—my heart
slicing like knives to protect my sinning self.

The one who surfaced flushed and late for prayers
at the bonfire, offering up each new lie
into the floating ashes. Crossing the river, the fear
is still fresh as I catch sight of a farmer, his hip
boots trudging, and buckets clanging over old corn stalks,
waist-high and wheat floating lazily into the Missouri.
And me, struck by how easy it is for him to stir the water,
surrounded by the deep spoiled pools.

CAFÉ IN OAKLAND

Sometimes the urge to live is carried in the sway
of a girl's hips
as she exits the coffee bar.

I don't even need to follow as she strolls
off in her Levi's.
I sit reading my paper,

thinking there is nothing new here, nothing
anyone can say to me
I'd find amusing, uplifting,

when someone in the corner leans over to light
a cigarette for a friend,
two lovers pour wine

from the little glass bottle, and I see a glint of it,
the tilt of a man's head
or a headline that looks promising

so I save it to read last, folding it
under my forearm to rest.

NOONTIME REVOLUTIONS

Sometimes the worst thing is to feel so ripe
with wine so light, the sea's a lucid sin
and with the hour only noon begins
when voices at the table's random flight
lift up in whimsy's sky to meet and soar,
and deep in concert with the landscape tune
to lower pitches of the tidal wounds.
And looking up, the rays of sun are poured
on men collecting tips from tables' hush
and onto loud machines that blow the leaves
and in the canvas that is when you see
the girl in foreground and the spreading moss
and realize what you thought was whispering
all those years was really shouting, shouting.

THE SPEED OF THE SKY

On a roof in Topeka, Kansas, a half-naked
Barbie Doll waves its legs at me as I stand
in my apartment window.

I had been looking for answers in the sky
of the gray morning, where clouds refused
to lift their humid veil.

At 40, I was waiting for them to tell me,
"Stop moaning and go to work", or maybe
"Call your ex and run back to the East Coast now!"

They say you can see forever here,
but the discarded Barbie Doll, legs up and stiff,
has taken me back to the David Street patio.

Tammy Kohler spreads her Barbie's arms
in triumph as she squeezes on her evening gown,
the sequins catching the Western Pennsylvania light.

I remember how at nine I thought those hills surrounding me
surrounded everything. I didn't yet know of Kansas'
sweeping vistas, how when the wind blew there was nothing to stop it.

I didn't know the speed of Chevy Lasers that boys revved
and how they flew down highways and into places
I wished were home.

How the broken down diners along the way
never lived up to the romantic dramas I'd played out,
restless, all that last summer at home.

Somewhere on Route 70, I'd end up calling,
breathless, from the closed payphone booth,
mouthing *"Please"* and *"Forgive me"* and *"Come now."*

It was the first time I thought about longing,
and how the things you've wanted
can bring you to regret.

Now, in apartment 909 in Topeka, Kansas I stand
in the window alone, measuring the speed of clouds,
945 miles from mornings of cereal and soccer.

Tammy broke the arms of her Barbie that summer.
She took trash to the curb and did dishes three times
a day saving up for a new model.

I wonder if there is a girl in the next apartment building,
and if she followed her mother to the roof one day with
wash in hand and too many dolls stuffed in a bag.

I wonder how this one is not missed,
where her evening dresses are hanging
and how long she will lie there naked looking up

to Topeka's unforgiving sky.

WHERE THE LILAC BUSH ONCE STOOD

In spring, mother carried in the short-lived blooms of the wild
bush at the alley's edge; carefully clipping the massive spray
of petals spread on the Formica table, leveling the water
in each tired vase. In twilight, she'd kneel to the neighbor's
back doors, leaving jarfuls in the dark film descending on David Street.
I'm visiting in June and the breeze of their lilac scent should be peaking
as I make the drive to the old house from my parent's "downsized" Cape Cod.
Bumping down the potholed pavement, I see lavender uprooted
for a parking pad and a lettered sign that warns not to trespass.
New people stare blankly at me as I step onto the familiar cracked sidewalk.
This house, the iron numerals "191" on the Dutch cellar door I touch, I feel
are mine, and I think they should know why I'm there—that I've come to claim
something left long ago in the faded bricks and cedar. Grown boys with keys
to Mustangs dangle their legs over the towering porch where I used to perch in the hazy
warm evenings, and I get that queasy feeling my mother felt when she saw me teetering
there and screamed *"Stay off the banister!"* Each night in her dreams
one of her four children must have tumbled from its ridges to the concrete.
Waiting for cars to pick me up and take me to places she'd never imagine,
I'd straddle there with my thighs in a delicate half-on, half-off balance
and nursed my far-off thoughts—foreign desires that took me as far away
as I could get from the lilac's aroma. But tonight something else is thickening
in the David Street air; it lingers heavy on my skin, as I back away
from the house, and into the fragrant spring night.

RETURN TO DAVID STREET, LATE SUMMER

Teenagers own this block and roam now,
barefoot and T-shirted in cigarette glow
like the fireflies I chased through this yard into darkness
with brothers too old to want me to tag along—
in Frisbee freeze games where we ran as fast
as we could and then stood stone still. All of us arching
our limbs like dying soldiers—Michael,
the alley boy, falling into the dirt-patched grass.
At dusk, he'd huddle behind our garage,
bringing city boys to poke sticks up my shorts.
I couldn't cry, standing above their smirks,
their idle bodies sitting bare-chested on the alley floor.
At night, I'd ease into the sting of hot water, scrub
off the day's gravel—images of boys rubbing
chew into their lips, lingering like the creaking sounds
of my parents outside on the patio swing.
Each night offered up its same glow
of flickering street lights,
the last chatter of porch talk fading,
as they faintly stirred the night air.
Tonight, the attic bedroom windows stick
as they're opened to sidewalk sounds
—metal and vibrating from an idling Impala.
Police car radios muffle cries of domestic calls.
In suffocating heat, my parents shut their windows
at night, knowing there's no seniority
in a block of aging structures, while I dream
of the little girl who said she'd never leave here.
Lying stiffly on the attic bed, covers off,
not even a sheet in the smoldering nightfall,
I listen to the street searing,
barely breathing.

THE PATTERN MAKER'S DAUGHTER

*"Students of Appalachian (geological) patterns have long puzzled over why some of
the main streams of the region depart now and then from the path of least resistance..."*
From *A Geography of Pennsylvania*

When you were born, father, and now
when you close your eyes to dream, it's the same
patterns blinking and repeating inside you,
steady as your infant first beats that tapped out
a precise rhythm, predictable as the projects
that came across your shop desk in the mill.

Beneath my shuttered eyelids, I've told you what I see—
the splits of our region's chaotic hills and stream—
our city's glittering dust particles breaking
from bedrock into the haphazard lines of my EEG—
the ones you willed to be more measured
as you sat amidst the bustle of Neurology waiting rooms.

We carry these innate flickerings, flashings
developed in our interior worlds, mine pulsing
like strobe patterns found in our ancient strata,
yours smooth as the flat rock at the bottom
of the Little Conemaugh—both of us shaped
by the igneous outcroppings penetrating our soft shale.

When my child was one day old we slept chest to chest
and I dreamed I was him. It was all I could do to pry
myself from that prism of color, shape, and constant
beat. I woke jolted and eyes open to the poor
beige of the room, the solid gray sheets.

Your patterns are worn into the grids of streets which
you walk each day, while I soar above the childhood alleys
I see when making love. I hover over the roof
of the vacuum repair shop, while underneath this city
lie the old tectonic forces, anxious and dendritic
—the random points I connect in poems that tie me to this earth.

Today when you sleep, you say you see the wood patterns
created in the shops of Bethlehem Steel, the racing algebra
of exacting molds—etched numerals you branded
into each piece with metal, and the countless 5 A.M.
eggs in a cup mother placed for you on the Formica table.

For me it's the intricate patterns of stream beds winding
across the black milk of my tedious slumber—tiny looping
lines that cross the topographic maps of Johnstown—
like the inking of electrodes I produced on paper.
They call to me from their brilliant beginnings—the Appalachian Plateau
I stretch in my dreams to meet—the orogeny of the Chestnut
and Laurel Mountains—howling and breaking off
as I twist and follow their endless, erratic passageways
beckoning and born from its ridges.

ACKNOWLEDGEMENTS

With thanks to these journals in which these poems have appeared or will appear:

Green Mountains Review, "Girl From Tanneryville, Johnstown Flood 1977";

Gargoyle Magazine, "Cures for Epilepsy, 500 B.C. to the Renaissance";

The Potomac Review, "Steeltown Girls" (Previously titled "Milltown Girls");

Poet Lore, "Prosperity, 1952";

The Ledge, "Café in Oakland";

Poetrymagazine.com, "Some Girls Have Auras of Bright Colors", "Stationary
     Front", "The Pattern Makers"

The Loyalhanna Review, "Johnstown Flood, 1977, The Day After";

Dark Lullaby, The Mekler Deahl (Hamilton Canada) Poetry Anthology of 2000,
     "The Bra Factory"

No Choice But to Trust, The Mekler Deahl Poetry Anthology of 1999; "I Can't
     Help But Think About Eve" First Prize and Winner of the
     Sandburg-Livesay Award Judged by Raymond Souster

"Waiting for you to Speak," The Meker Deahl Poetry Anthology of 1998,
     "The Secret";

Pittsburgh Post-Gazette: "In the Kitchen at the Greek Boy Diner" and
     "Hockey."

"Some Girls Have Auras of Bright Colors" placed third in the Chautauqua
Writer's Center Poetry Contest, Judged by Diane Hume George.
"Visit to Cohoes" (as "The Visit Home") placed Second in The Masters
Poetry Series Competition judged by Ed Ochester.

ABOUT THE AUTHOR

Sandee Gertz Umbach was born and raised in the tiny Borough of Dale, a urban "island" surrounded by the City of Johnstown, Pennsylvania. Here, she found endless inspiration as an adult writer and poet. She has worked for a news magazine in Washington, D.C. where she lived for several years before moving to Elmira, New York, and eventually settling south of Pittsburgh in Washington, PA, where she and her husband Paul raised two boys who both enjoy writing. Her son, Jordan, caught the bug for "steeltown lore" and is a singer/songwriter with many songs reflecting Western Pennsylvania heritage.

The author is a Commonwealth Speaker with the Pennsylvania Humanities Council where she leads poetry workshops that focus on a sense of place. She founded and President of the award-winning non-profit arts center, The Washington Community Arts and Cultural Center in Washington, PA which provides fine arts programming for children and youth. Each summer, she returns to Dale Borough to the Dale Valley Arts Center where she teaches poetry to children in a program she developed entitled "My Own Backyard." She has a Masters of Arts in Creative Writing from the Wilkes University Low-Residency Program and is currently an M.F.A. candidate. She received a poetry fellowship from the Pennsylvania Council on the Arts in 2000.

The quote below has been integral to her inspiration in writing about the theme of her father's work. This is obvious in the poem "The Pattern Makers." The concept of a pattern maker possessing a "duality" of math/science and art. "To see the finished product…to see things no one else sees…"

"To be a successful machine pattern maker, one must be expert in interpreting the ideas of the designer as indicated by the drawings and sketches, and he should be able to visualize what is represented in order to see the finished job at the start and work from both his and the molder's point of view." *Joseph A. Shelly, Author of Pattern Making, 1920*

RECENT BOOKS BY
BOTTOM DOG PRESS

WORKING LIVES SERIES
The Way-Back Room: Memoir of a Detroit Childhood
by Mary Minock, 216 pgs. $18
The Free Farm: A Novel by Larry Smith
306 pgs. $18
Sinners of Sanction County: Stories by Charles Dodd White
160 pgs. $17
Learning How: Stories, Yarns & Tales by Richard Hague
216 pgs. $18
Strangers in America: A Novel by Erika Meyers
140 pgs. $16
Riders on the Storm: A Novel by Susan Streeter Carpenter
404 pgs. $18
The Long River Home by Larry Smith
230 pgs. cloth $22; paper $16
Landscape with Fragmented Figures by Jeff Vande Zande
232 pgs. $16
The Big Book of Daniel: Collected Poems by Daniel Thompson
340 pgs. cloth $22; paper $18
Reply to an Eviction Notice: Poems by Robert Flanagan
100 pgs. $15
An Unmistakable Shade of Red & The Obama Chronicles
by Mary E. Weems, 80 pgs. $15
d.a.levy & the mimeograph revolution eds. Ingrid Swanberg
& Larry Smith, 276 pgs. & dvd $25
Our Way of Life: Poems by Ray McNiece
128 pgs. $14

ANTHOLOGIES:
Degrees of Elevation: Short Stories of Contemporary Appalachia
eds. Charles Dodd White & Page Seay 186 pgs. $18
On the Clock: Contemporary Short Stories of Work
eds. Josh Maday & Jeff Vande Zande 226 pgs. $18

BOTTOM DOG PRESS
http://smithdocs.net

OTHER BOOKS BY
BIRD DOG PUBLISHING

A Poetic Journey, Poems by Robert A. Reynolds
86 pgs. $16
Dogs and Other Poems by Paul Piper
80 pgs. $15
The Mermaid Translation by Allen Frost
140 pgs. $15
Heart Murmurs: Poems by John Vanek
120 pgs. $15
Home Recordings: Tales and Poems by Allen Frost
$14
A Life in Poems by William C. Wright
$10
Faces and Voices: Tales by Larry Smith
136 pgs. $14
Second Story Woman: A Memoir of Second Chances
by Carole Calladine, 226 pgs. $15
256 Zones of Gray: Poems by Rob Smith
80 pgs. $14
Another Life: Collected Poems by Allen Frost
176 pgs. $14
Winter Apples: Poems by Paul S. Piper
88 pgs. $14
Lake Effect: Poems by Laura Treacy Bentley
108 pgs. $14
Depression Days on an Appalachian Farm: Poems
by Robert L. Tener, 80 pgs. $14
120 Charles Street, The Village: Journals & Other Writings 1949-1950
by Holly Beye, 240 pgs. $15

BIRD DOG PUBLISHING
A division of Bottom Dog Press, Inc.
Order Online at:
http://smithdocs.net/BirdDogy/BirdDogPage.html

CPSIA information can be obtained at www.ICGtesting.com
Printed in the USA
BVOW011422250112

281328BV00001BA/35/P